CONCEPT CARS

Motor Mania

by Jeffrey Zuehlke

Mike Mueller, consultant and automotive writer and photographer

Lerner Publications Company • Minneapolis

Lerner Publications Company
A division of Lerner Publishing Group
241 First Avenue North
Minneapolis, MN 55401 U.S.A.

Website address: www.lernerbooks.com

Library of Congress Cataloging-in-Publication Data

Zuehlke, Jeffrey, 1968–
        Concept cars / by Jeffrey Zuehlke.
        p.   cm. — (Motor mania)
        Includes bibliographical references and index.
        ISBN-13: 978–0–8225–6568–0 (lib. bdg. : alk. paper)
        ISBN-10: 0–8225–6568–4 (lib. bdg. : alk. paper)
        1. Experimental automobiles—Juvenile literature. I. Title.
        TL147.Z837 2007
        629.222—dc22   2006018805

Manufactured in the United States of America
1 2 3 4 5 6 – DP – 12 11 10 09 08 07

Contents

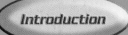

Introduction

What's new? What's next? How far can we go? These are the questions car designers ask when they dream up concept cars.

Concept cars are idea cars, dream cars, *wow* cars. They aren't built for sale to the public. Many don't even run. And only a few concept cars ever go on to be mass-produced (built in large numbers).

Why would an automaker spend millions of dollars to build a car that no one will ever buy or drive? Because concept cars are all about the future. They are a way for car designers to try new ideas and new technology. They are a way for automakers to show what their cars of the future might look like. Most of all, concept cars are about creating excitement—the wow factor. They are built to create a buzz.

Concept cars are introduced and displayed at auto shows around the world. They draw crowds and get people talking. They generate magazine and newspaper articles and television news stories. Concept cars are a mix of the latest technology and showmanship. They get people excited about cars and excited about the future.

For its 75th anniversary, Italian design company Pininfarina worked with Italian carmaker Maserati on the 2005 Birdcage 75 concept car. This stunning dream car featured a 700-horsepower V12 engine, a carbon fiber body, and infrared cameras.

Chapter One

CONCEPT CAR HISTORY

The 1896 Duryea *(below)* was built by the Duryea Motor Wagon Company, the first U.S. automaker.

No single person invented the automobile. In the late 1800s, many inventors in both Europe and the United States were working to build "horseless carriages," or automobiles. It took years of trial and error to design and build cars that worked well.

By the early 1900s, the automaking industry had grown quickly. Many small companies were born then. A handful of them grew into industry powerhouses. They include the Ford Motor Company, founded by Henry Ford in Dearborn, Michigan, in 1903.

William C. Durant created General Motors (GM) in 1908 in Detroit, Michigan. These two companies would go on to become two of the largest businesses in the world. Walter P. Chrysler's Chrysler Corporation started in 1925. His company later joined the other two to form the "Big Three" U.S. automakers. While smaller automakers came and went over the years, the Big Three ruled the U.S. automotive industry.

Different Companies, Different Ideas

By the 1920s, Ford and GM had developed very different ideas about how to sell cars to the U.S. public. Years earlier, Henry Ford had created the Model T. This simple, no-nonsense car

Ford Motor Company's Model T was one of the most important automobiles of the early 1900s. It was produced from 1908 to 1927 with few design changes. This is a 1919 model.

Car styling changed greatly in the 1900s. Here is a 1920 Packard sedan *(left)* next to an older, carriage-style automobile. Note how the carriage-style car looked a bit like a carriage drawn by a horse.

was a huge hit. Ford sold millions of Model Ts in the first decades of the 1900s on his way to becoming the largest automaker in the world. But as the years passed, Ford made very few changes to the car. For example, most Model Ts came in one color—black. By the 1920s, the Model T had become boring and outdated.

Meanwhile, Alfred P. Sloan, the head of GM, was taking his company in a different direction. Sloan understood

that good cars weren't enough for the U.S. public anymore. By the 1920s, cars were a huge part of American life. They were more than just a way to get around. They were a way for Americans to express their personalities and identities. For example, a young college graduate probably wouldn't be interested in the same kind of car as a wealthy, older gentleman.

With this idea in mind, GM owned several divisions, or brands, of cars. It carefully tailored each brand to fit certain types of buyers. GM's Chevrolet division (often nicknamed Chevy) specialized in simple cars that were affordable. On the other end of the GM brand list was Cadillac. Cadillacs were the ultimate luxury vehicles. They featured all the newest ideas and technology. They were also very expensive. Cadillacs were made for rich people who wanted the best and fanciest cars available. GM designed its other brands—Pontiac, Buick, and Oldsmobile—to fit in between

Chevrolet and Cadillac. GM had products that appealed to just about any car-buying American.

This strategy wasn't GM's only important idea. The concept of planned obsolescence also changed how cars were built and sold. (*Obsolescence* is related to the word *obsolete*. The word *obsolete* means "out of date" or "no longer in use.") GM came up with the idea of making improvements to their cars each year. Sometimes the changes were small. For example, a new model might have the same basic body as last year's model. The small changes might include a slightly different front grille or a different shape to the taillights. Every few years, cars would get major redesigns to keep them looking fresh and new.

The changes would make last year's cars seem out of date. The improvements would also keep the public eager to see what was coming next. Best of all for GM, the changes would encourage people to buy a new car more often—just to have the newest and latest thing. Planned obsolescence was a huge key to GM's success. In the 1920s, GM topped Ford as the world's largest automaker.

Harley Earl and the LaSalle

The man in charge of keeping GM's models looking fresh, new, and exciting

Harley Earl

Harley Earl *(right)* (1893–1969) is the most famous automobile designer in U.S. history. He worked for GM from 1927 to 1959. He and his design team created some of the greatest classic cars of all time. They include the Corvette and the famous Cadillacs of the years after World War II. Earl introduced many car design innovations, such as chrome trim, two-tone paint jobs, wraparound windshields, and tail fins.

was Harley Earl. Earl had made a name for himself designing and building coachwork (specially made car bodies) for movie stars in Hollywood, California. GM's top bosses had seen Earl's work and invited him to design cars for the company.

Earl's first effort for GM was the 1927 LaSalle. The LaSalle was one of the first mass-produced cars that made looks a big priority. Before then, automobiles didn't have much style. They were like boxes on wheels. Cars had a box that covered the engine, a box for the passengers to sit in, and a box for storage.

The LaSalle was much more than that. Its front fenders sloped gracefully down to the running boards (footboards below the doors on the outside of an automobile). The LaSalle also featured a gleaming front grille and a stylish, two-color paint job. Earl's graceful machine pointed the U.S. car industry in a new direction.

The Y-Job

As head of GM's Art and Color Section, Earl brought style and personality to all of GM's brands and cars. GM's focus on style and planned obsolescence forced the rest of the automotive industry to work to keep up.

Meanwhile, improvements to car technology and styling kept coming. In the mid-1930s, Earl decided to build a special car that would point the way toward the future. It would bring together many of the best ideas for future cars. The car was named the Buick Y-Job.

Why the "Y-Job"?

The Y-Job's name came from the aircraft industry. Aircraft makers used the letter X in the names of their experimental machines (for example, the X-15). They used the letter Y for their most advanced and radical machines. So calling the car the Y-Job was Earl's way of saying his car was on the cutting edge of technology.

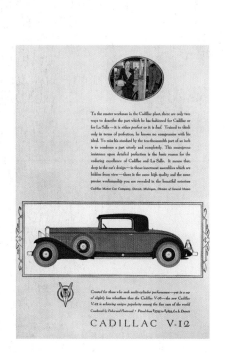

To the master workman in the Cadillac plant, there are only two ways to describe the part which he has fashioned for Cadillac or for LaSalle—it is either *perfect* or it is *bad*. Trained to think only in terms of perfection, he knows no compromise with his ideal. To miss his standard by the ten-thousandth part of an inch is to condemn a part utterly and completely. This courageous insistence upon detailed perfection is the basic reason for the enduring excellence of Cadillac and LaSalle. It means that, deep in the car's design—in those innermost assemblies which are hidden from view—there is the same high quality and the same precise workmanship you see revealed in the beautiful exteriors

Cadillac Motor Car Company, Detroit, Michigan, Division of General Motors

Created for those who seek multi-cylinder performance—yet is a car of slightly less wheelbase than the Cadillac V-16—the new Cadillac V-12 is achieving unique popularity among the fine cars of the world Coachwork by Fisher and Fleetwood • Priced from $3795 to $4895, f.o.b. Detroit

CADILLAC V-12

This advertisement explained the features of the Cadillac V12 and the LaSalle.

The Y-Job had many new features. It had a convertible top that opened and closed with the push of a button. (Back in the 1930s, convertibles had to be opened and closed by hand.) The car also had power windows—another first. And it had hidden headlights that swiveled out of sight when turned off. The Y-Job's amazing features would become common on modern cars.

New technology was only part of the Y-Job's appeal. The car's smooth, graceful styling was far ahead of its time. The Y-Job had no running boards. Its rounded fenders blended in with the rest of the body. Overall, the car had a long, low, sleek, and futuristic look.

GM sent the Y-Job on a tour around the country. It appeared at auto shows—events where automakers showed off their newest models. The Y-Job was a big hit. The concept car was born. Although only one Y-Job was ever built, its low, sleek look would later inspire production car design.

Chrysler's First Concept Cars

The Chrysler Corporation soon started building its own concept cars. In 1941 the company unveiled the Thunderbolt and the Newport. Chrysler called the strangely shaped Thunderbolt the Car of the Future.

Harley Earl sits in the 1938 Buick Y-Job, which he designed. The Y–Job was a fully operational vehicle. Earl often drove it to work at GM.

Like the Y-Job, it had hidden head-lights and a power convertible roof. But the Thunderbolt's wide, fat body looked even more futuristic than the Y-Job. The Newport was a very long and elegant machine. Its most unusual feature was its separate front and back passenger compartments. To show them off to car buyers, Chrysler built six copies of each machine and sent them on tours around the country. But Chrysler chose not to mass pro-duce any of its first concept cars.

GM and Chrysler had to put their concept car plans on hold, however,

when the United States entered World War II (1939–1945) in 1941. All U.S. car-makers stopped producing cars during the war. Instead, they built weapons and vehicles for the war effort. After the war ended, the companies needed some time to get back on track.

Motoramas and the Golden Age of Concept Cars

By 1949 the Big Three were hard at work making new cars for an eager public. To drum up even more excite-ment, GM held a huge show in 1949. GM put all its new cars on display at

The 1941 Chrysler Newport had two folding windshields but no side windows or mirrors. The fenders on its aluminum body hid part of the rear wheels.

the fancy Waldorf-Astoria Hotel in New York City. GM held a second show in Boston. The events created a huge buzz, and nearly 600,000 people attended. The show was such a success that GM held several more in the coming years. The events would come to be known as the General Motors Motoramas. They were a perfect place to introduce the company's newest cars—and wildest concept machines.

At GM's 1953 Motorama in New York City, visitors could get a peek at thirty-eight new models. They were also treated to orchestra, choir, and ballet performances and a fashion show.

Ford's first concept car was the X–100.

One of the most memorable GM concepts was the 1951 Buick LeSabre. This creation looked like a cross between a car and a fighter jet. The LeSabre's body had smooth, rounded edges and tail fins that looked as if they had been taken from an airplane. The LeSabre's tail cone looked like the rear of a jet engine. In addition to its looks, the LeSabre boasted new technology. For example, a device on the car automatically closed the convertible top when it sensed rain.

Meanwhile, Chrysler was hard at work developing a new set of concepts. The company joined forces with an Italian company, Ghia. In the coming years, Chrysler and Ghia produced many stunning concept cars. One of the best was the 1951 Chrysler K-310, a large and shapely luxury car.

That year Ford finally got into the concept car act. The X-100's jetlike styling was similar to the LeSabre. The driver's compartment looked like a cockpit, and the front of the car looked like a rocket ship. Ford's new concept brought the company some attention. But GM's concepts would continue to lead the way in the 1950s.

At the 1953 Motorama, GM showed a concept for a roadster—a small convertible sports car. The nifty little Corvette was such a hit that GM decided to build the car for the public. The Chevrolet Corvette has gone on to become one of the most famous American cars. Nevertheless, the Corvette was tame compared to some of GM's other creations of the 1950s.

In 1954 the company unveiled the first Firebird concept car. This unusual jet-powered machine was more or less an airplane without wings. The driver sat in a small cockpit that was covered with a bubble-shaped plastic canopy—just like in a fighter plane. The Firebird was too strange to ever be mass-produced. But it created plenty of buzz for GM. In the coming years, the company went on to build the Firebird II and the Firebird III. Each car was wilder than the last. The Firebird III had no steering wheel. Instead, the drivers used joysticks to steer the car.

American automakers weren't the only ones producing concept cars. Italian coach builder Bertone built a series of shapely sports cars for Italian carmaker Alfa Romeo. Known as the BAT cars, the machines had smooth, rounded bodies and tall, curving tail fins. They were designed to be aero-dynamic—to glide through the air as easily as possible. Like the Firebirds, the BAT cars were just experiments. They were never meant to be sold to the public.

GM came out with the 1954 Firebird I *(left)*, the 1956 Firebird II *(center)*, and the 1959 Firebird III *(right)*. They were built to test the possibility of using gas turbine engines in cars. These high-powered engines are used in aircraft and large land vehicles, such as tanks.

The 1969 Chevy Manta Ray was really a redesigned Mako Shark II.

Concepts of the 1960s and 1970s

Harley Earl retired in 1959, and GM staged its last Motorama in 1961. The concept craze began to fade in the United States. U.S. automakers continued to build concepts to show off to the public. But the wild designs of the 1950s gave way to more realistic ideas.

One of the most memorable concepts of the 1960s was the 1961 Mako Shark. It was named after a real kind of shark. The Mako was a sleek Corvette with sharklike details. Its front end was long and flat, like a shark's nose. Exhaust pipes flowed out of gill-like holes in the side. The Mako Shark's paint scheme even matched the blue, gray, and white coloring of a real mako shark. The car was dark blue on top but faded to a cool gray and then white on the bottom.

In the 1970s, world events and new laws put a dent in concept car design. A series of oil shortages led to sky-high gas prices. Automakers put their energies into designing smaller cars that used less gas.

Other new laws pushed car companies to build safer cars. This left little time to dream up amazing concept cars. "Most designers consider the '70s a lost decade," says Bill Porter, who designed cars for GM at the time.

Yet concept cars remained a big deal in Europe, with many unusual machines appearing. For example, the Italian design company Pininfarina worked with Italian carmaker Ferrari to build the Modulo, a very low and streamlined car with a futuristic shape. German carmaker Mercedes-Benz created a series of sleek, high-powered sports cars known as the C 111s. One

C 111 topped 250 miles (402 kilometers) per hour in speed tests.

Modern Concept Cars: The 1980s to the 2000s

By the 1980s, things were beginning to look up for U.S. automakers. The Big Three began to take a new interest in building concepts. Ford took the lead, introducing the Probe series. These angular cars were designed to be very fuel efficient.

Many concept cars of the 1980s and 1990s wound up becoming production

The C 111 was as fast as a race car with all the comforts of a luxury car. Its gull wing doors opened straight up, like the wings of a seagull.

cars. Chrysler created a sensation in the 1980s when it launched one of the world's great concept cars—the Dodge Viper. This low and shapely sports car had killer looks and a massive V10 engine. The Viper created so much excitement that Chrysler soon began building them for the public.

In 1990 Chrysler came up with a very different—but still wild—concept. The Voyager III was actually two vehicles. One part was a small, three-seat car. The second part was a large passenger compartment that held eight people. The two pieces could be attached to make a large minivan. This clever machine never made it into production, however.

Outside the United States, German automaker Volkswagen introduced a cute little bug-shaped car in 1994. Concept I was an updated version of the famous Volkswagen Beetle. The car was such a hit that Volkswagen made plans to mass-produce the car. And the highly popular New Beetle was born.

The 1993 Dodge Viper RT/10 was one of the models produced as a result of the popularity of the 1989 Viper concept car.

In 1998 Chrysler showcased the Pronto Cruizer, a snazzy coupe. The car's rounded shape reminded many of classic cars from the 1930s. People liked it so much that Chrysler began producing it as the PT Cruiser.

The Pronto Cruizer (*pictured*) was the concept car behind the wildly popular PT Cruiser produced in the early 2000s.

Toyota's POD was designed with the latest technology to respond to the moods of the driver and passengers. Its onboard computer even takes a picture of the riders when it senses that everyone inside is laughing and having a good time!

The 2000s brought some of the most creative concepts yet. Many of the wildest designs have come from Japanese automakers. For example, the Honda Unibox is a box-shaped minivan with six wheels. The peculiar machine has see-through body panels. Two foldable electric motorcycles can be stowed inside the doors.

Toyota's 2001 POD concept is more than just a car. The cute, boxy four-seater is almost like a member of the family. The POD features a computer system that adjusts to the driver's feelings. It keeps track of the driver's heartbeat and how much he or she is sweating. If the driver is showing signs of being upset, the POD blows cool air and plays relaxing music. The idea is that a calm, happy driver is a safe driver.

The POD also shows the driver's feelings to other drivers on the road. Lights on the front of the car change color to express the driver's mood. When the driver slams on the brakes, the front lights turn red to express anger. The lights turn dark blue when the driver is sad—for example, when the car runs out of gas. The POD even has a little tail in back that wags like a dog's tail. The idea is that allowing drivers to communicate with one another will reduce accidents and make roads and highways safer.

The POD may sound like a wild idea, but it's not too far from reality. Toyota is working to develop the POD's systems for everyday cars. Like so many concept cars before it, the

Concepts vs. Production Cars

Dreaming up concepts is different from designing cars for mass production. For production cars, designers need to think about more than style. Building a new production car means designing every part of the car down to the last detail. It means tooling—setting up the factory to build the car. Designing a new production car means ordering materials (such as steel and plastic) from outside sources. It's a huge, expensive job that costs hundreds of millions of dollars. It's also very risky because those millions could be wasted if the car turns out to be a flop.

This is one of the great uses of concept cars. Concepts are a great way to test a new car to see what people think of it. If people like it, the car may go into production. If the car proves unpopular, the company can toss the idea away. The company only spent money building one or a few vehicles instead of thousands.

POD is more than just a fun idea. It's a look into the future.

At the same time, some automakers have looked to the past to find ideas for future cars. In 2003 Ford introduced a concept for a redesigned model of its popular Mustang. The concept reminded many of the very first Mustangs from the 1960s. The new "retro" Mustang went into production in 2005 and has been popular with buyers.

The Mustang's success inspired GM and Chrysler. Both companies designed retro versions of cars that were popular in the 1960s and 1970s. In 2006 Chevrolet unveiled a concept for a new Camaro. Meanwhile, Dodge (part of DaimlerChrysler) showed off its Challenger concept. Both cars feature a stylish mix of retro and modern. The Challenger will go into production in 2008. The Camaro will follow in 2009. For concept car designers, great ideas can come from the past or the future.

Chapter Two

CREATING CONCEPT CARS

What goes into designing and building a concept car? It's a very complicated mix of art and science.

"A car is made up of hundreds of developments of different kinds of technology, from lighting systems . . . seating systems to steering systems and on and on and on," says Freeman Thomas. (He helped design the Volkswagen Concept I.) The designer's job is to fit this technology into an attractive package that will excite the public.

Most concept cars start out as clay, plastic, or metal models *(right)*. A small number are made into full-size models. Fewer still become fully working vehicles.

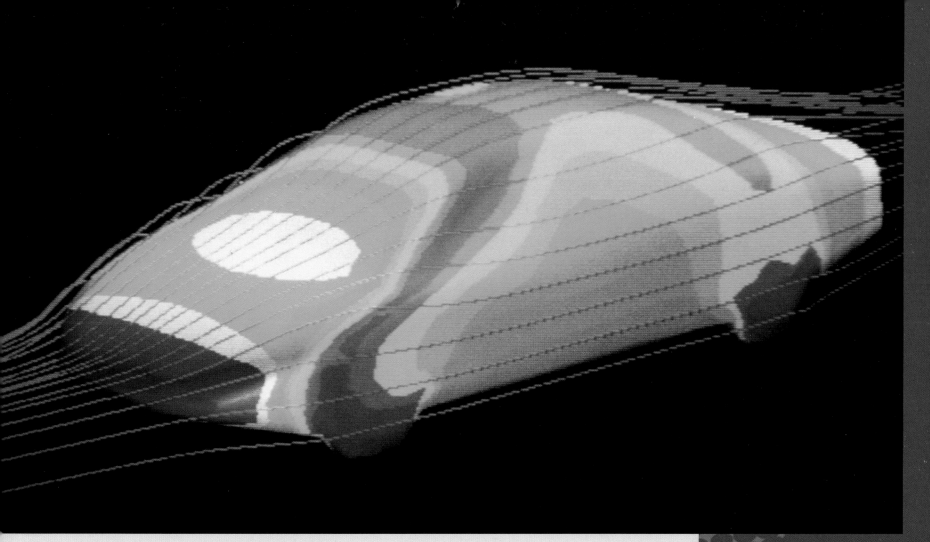

Becoming a Car Designer

Car designers must have a strong education in both science and art. Designers must understand how cars work. They must know about all the different systems found in cars and where those systems can be placed. Car designers also must understand scientific ideas such as aerodynamics. This is the study of how things move through the air. Aerodynamics has a big effect on how a car will perform on the road. Designers also need to know the history of cars—how cars looked and worked in the past. They use this knowledge to see what has worked—and not worked—before.

Car designers can use computers to test the aerodynamics of a new car design. The dashed lines on this computer-generated image show how air will move over and around the car when it is in motion.

Car designers must know what the public likes and wants. They must stay on top of the latest trends—from clothing to television shows. They need to keep their ideas fresh and exciting. They also need to have a sense of what people might like in the future. Most designers are dreaming up cars that won't be seen or sold for at least a few years, if not longer.

Another important design skill is the ability to communicate ideas. Designers must be able to turn their visions into reality. This means drawing sketches, creating illustrations on computers, and building clay models. Then they use the illustrations and models to build full-size cars. It's a challenging job—but an exciting one.

Most designers learn their trade at design schools. These colleges specialize in the different skills of design, such as drawing and creating models. One of the best car design programs is at the Art Center College of Design in Pasadena, California. The College

for Creative Design in Detroit, Michigan, and the Royal College of Art in Britain also have strong programs. At these and other schools, students learn more than just how to design cool-looking car bodies. They also spend a lot of their time on the details. They sketch everything from door handles to windshield wipers to headlights.

Students graduate with the skills they need to work in automotive design. From there, they will look for a job with a design studio of one of the world's major automakers, such as GM, Ford, Toyota, Honda, or BMW. They might also be lucky enough to land a job at the famous Italian design houses Pininfarina or Bertone.

DID YOU KNOW?
About half of the world's car designers have come from Pasadena's Art Center College of Design.

24

A student at the College for Creative Design in Detroit, Michigan, works on sketches for a new car design.

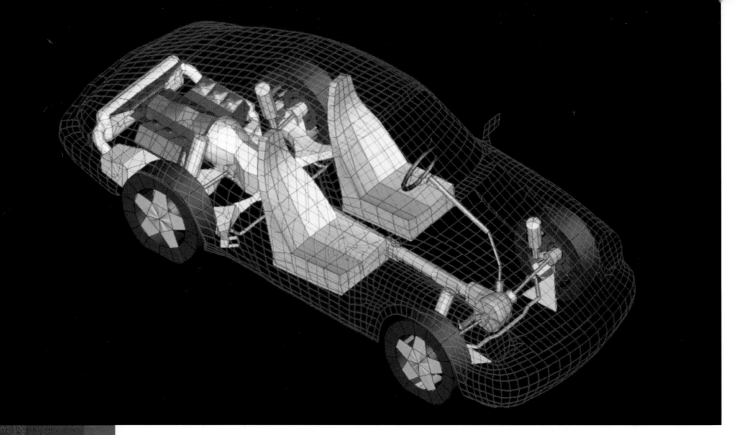

CAD software allows designers to see how the mechanical parts of a car will fit into a new car design.

From Idea to Machine

Every concept car starts out as an idea—a vision in the designer's head. Bringing that idea to life is a long process that requires a lot of thought and effort.

Most designers start out by sketching their idea on paper. They begin with a very rough sketch and then work on many drafts. The drawings help them to sort out the details. Designers make sketches of the doors, the trunk, the interior, the seats, and the dashboard—just about every part of the car. They also make drawings of the car from many different angles—front views, rear views, side views, overhead views. Slowly, the car begins to take shape.

After finishing the sketches, the next step is to create a computer model of the car. To do this, designers use special computer-aided design (CAD) software. AutoStudio is one such program. It takes a designer's sketches and turns them into

3-D images that can be viewed from any angle on a computer screen. Using CAD programs, the designer can make and view changes to the design in seconds. The designer can experiment with different colors, shapes, and details to get a picture of what the car will look like.

But computer programs can only do so much. Seeing a car on the screen does not bring it to life. "We're not comfortable designing completely in the computer simply because you don't have the ability to walk around the car in real time,"

says J Mays, the head of design at Ford Motor Company. "We simply don't have a big enough screen to accurately portray the size of something like an automobile." And so comes the next stage of design—the clay model.

Sculpting a Concept: Clay Models

For decades, car designers have used clay models to test their designs in three dimensions. Using clay allows designers to make changes as they work without having to start from scratch.

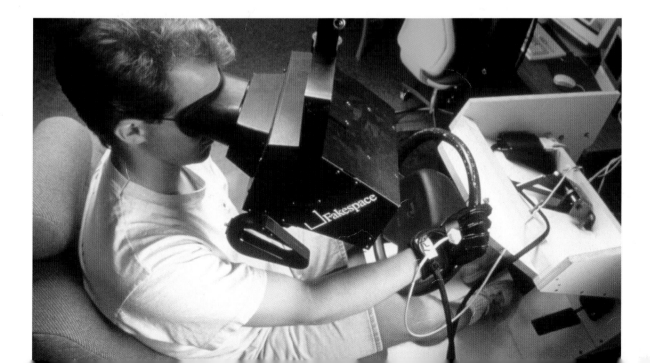

Virtual reality car design is being used more and more in car design. It is cheaper than building the car, and the designer can experience the design of the car.

Car Design Lingo

Car designers have specific names to describe different sections of a vehicle. Designers can change the look and performance of a car by changing the design of these features.

beltline: the line running around a car's body. The beltline is formed by the bottom edges of the car's windows.

DLO: "daylight opening," or window

greenhouse: the section of a car's body that rises above the beltline of the car. The greenhouse is the upper part of the passenger area that contains the DLOs (windows).

pillars: posts on the greenhouse of the car that support the roof. The pillars closest to the windshield are called A-pillars, and the ones nearest the rear window are C- or D-pillars. The posts on the side of the car in between the other pillars are called B-pillars.

rocker panel: the section of a vehicle body that is between the front and rear fenders and beneath the doors

wheel arch: the opening around the wheel of a vehicle that is formed by the edge of the fender

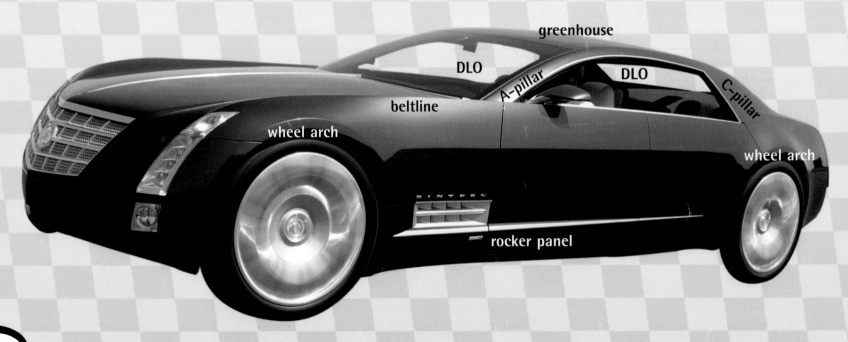

For each car, designers usually build a handful of models of different sizes. For example, they will often build one at one-fifth scale (one-fifth the size of a real car), two-fifths scale, and full size. To build a model, designers begin by building a frame in the rough shape of the car. This foam or plywood frame is called the buck. After the buck is completed, designers apply a thin layer of clay.

Up to this point, the process is very similar to how cars were designed

Harley Earl, Sculptor

Legend has it that Harley Earl was the first car designer to use clay models to help with designing cars. Some even say that Earl dug up his own clay from the banks of a California stream.

back in the days of Harley Earl. But modern technology has made shaping much easier and more precise. Large and expensive robots, known as milling machines, help with the details.

CONCEPT CAR TERM

Blue-sky vehicle: a design in which the sky is the limit. This means an automaker has no plans to put the car into production, so designers are free to try new and unusual ideas.

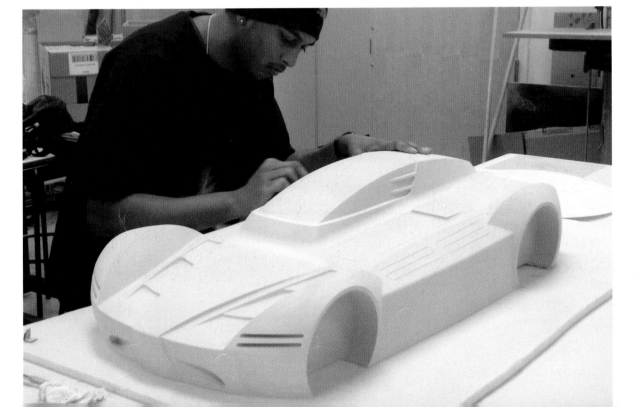

A car design student carves exterior details into a clay model.

Designers program the machines to sculpt the model to match their computer design. The result is a perfect clay model.

Once the sculpting is done, the design team paints the car. Custom-made parts, such as door handles, lights, and chrome trim are some of the last things to be added. After months or years of work, the designer's idea has become a 3-D object. The next step is to show the models to other people in the company to get their reaction.

GM Technical Center

GM does much of its design at the General Motors Technical Center. Its campus was built in the 1950s and is located 12 miles (19 km) north of Detroit, Michigan. The massive center includes 25 buildings on 330 acres (133 hectares).

If the model gets the go-ahead, it will be made into a concept car and shown off at auto shows around the world.

A senior transportation design student presents a design for a new automobile.

Damsels of Design

For most of its history, the auto industry has been run by men. Women had few opportunities to make an impact on how cars were designed and built. Yet by the 1950s, studies had shown that women often played a key role in choosing their family's car. Harley Earl hired women for his design staff in the mid-1950s. He felt that women designers would have the best ideas for making cars that appealed to women. The team was given the nickname the Damsels of Design. Earl's group began by helping to design car interiors. But they were never given a chance to have an impact on overall car design, and the team was broken up after Earl's retirement in 1959. In the 1950s and 1960s, women simply weren't welcomed into such influential roles in a male-dominated industry. This attitude has changed in recent decades. In the 2000s, women have far more opportunities in the auto industry.

These six women and three others were known as the Damsels of Design.

Auto Shows

Auto shows are huge events in the car industry. They are a way for automakers to show off their newest products to the media and the public. Like the old GM Motoramas, the major auto shows are glitzy affairs. They feature live music, celebrities, and tons of glamour and excitement.

The biggest auto shows in the United States are held in Detroit, Michigan; Los Angeles, California; and New York City, New York. Frankfurt, Germany; Geneva, Switzerland; and Tokyo, Japan, host the most important shows overseas. All the world's top automakers bring their newest concept cars and newest production vehicles to these shows. Thousands of smaller auto shows take place in cities all over the world.

Most automakers bring at least two or three concepts to the big shows. They unveil the new machines on

Visitors to the 2004 International Motor Show in Geneva, Switzerland, check out the latest models and concept car designs.

A crowd gathers to check out the 2003 Ford Mustang GT Coupe concept car at an auto show in Detroit, Michigan.

stage under bright lights with lots of hype. Visitors purchase tickets for the chance to wander around the show and view the new cars. The car companies carefully keep track of the public's reaction to their new concepts. If a concept car doesn't thrill the crowd, the automaker knows it has a dud. However, if a concept is a hit, the company will think about taking the huge step from concept to production car. This process—of building something new and testing it with the public—is what concept cars are all about.

DID YOU KNOW?
Most automakers spend $100 million or more on their car design departments each year.

1938 Buick Y-Job

Harley Earl's famous Y-Job was years ahead of its time. It included new features such as power windows and a powered convertible top. The Y-Job also was the first car with "hidden" headlights that flipped out of sight when the car's lights turned off. Earl's machine also had futuristic styling. Its sleek, low look would be seen on production cars of the 1940s and 1950s. Earl used the Y-Job as his regular car for many years.

1951 Buick LeSabre

The years after World War II are sometimes called the jet age. Aircraft makers were using the first jet engines. These new engines pushed aircraft to record speeds. Harley Earl's car was named after the F-86 Sabre, one of the very first U.S. Air Force jet fighter planes. The LeSabre's styling was based on jet aircraft. The oval on the front hood looks like a jet's front air intake. The rear of the car has airplane-like tail fins and a large hole in back that looks like a jet engine's exhaust.

1954 Alfa Romeo BAT 7

BAT 7 is the second of three concept cars created by Italian design company Bertone in the 1950s. Like the BAT 5 and BAT 9, BAT 7 was an experiment in aerodynamics. In fact, BAT stands for "Berlinetta (small sedan) Aerodinamica (aerodynamic) Tecnica (technique)." Italian automaker Alfa Romeo asked Bertone to build the cars to see how aerodynamics affected a car's performance. The BAT 7 is the most extraordinary of the three, with radically curved rear wings.

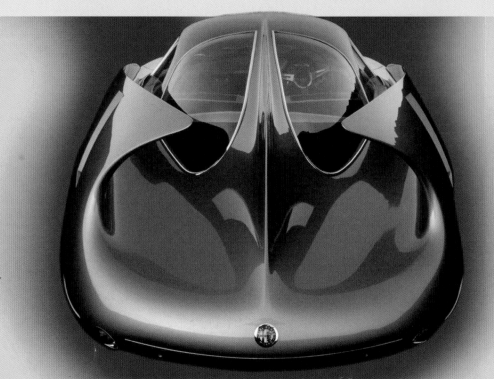

1957 Ford Nucleon

Ford's Nucleon was not a full-size car. Instead, Ford built a three-eighths scale model to show off its ideas. The Nucleon was meant to be powered by a small nuclear reactor, the kind used in nuclear power plants. Since nuclear reactors become dangerously hot, Ford's designers set the engine in the rear of the car, separate from the passengers. No nuclear-powered cars have ever been built. Fifty years later, the Nucleon is still far ahead of its time.

1961 Chevrolet Mako Shark

Legend has it that GM design chief Bill Mitchell came up with the idea for this car while deep-sea fishing. After catching a small shark, Mitchell was inspired by the animal's unique shape, features, and colors. These features appear on the Mako Shark. The wide and flat front end is similar to a shark's. The slats in front of and behind the front wheels look like gills. The car's gray and blue paint scheme also match the color of the animal. Many of these stunning details began appearing on Corvettes of the mid-1960s.

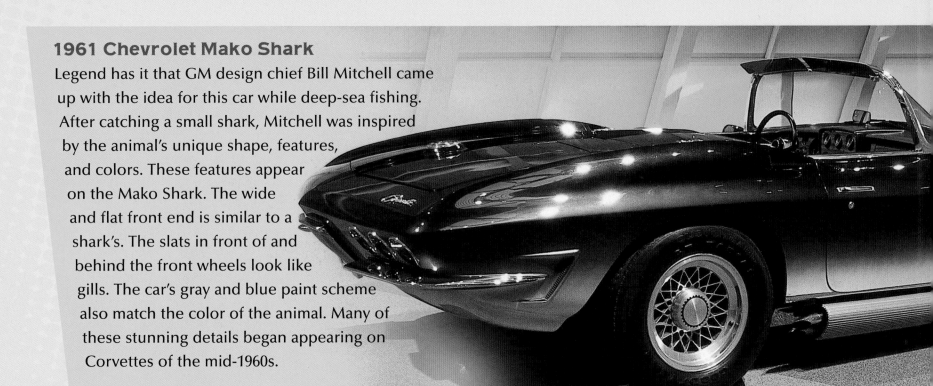

1970 Bertone Stratos

The wedge-shaped Stratos was certainly cutting edge. It was also completely impractical as a road car. Bertone's concept was just 33 inches (84 cm) tall. The passenger compartment was tiny, and the car had no side doors. Instead, the windshield could be opened, allowing rider and driver to get in and out. Its engine was in the back, so the car had no rear window or visibility. In 1974 Italian carmaker Lancia introduced a watered-down version of the car as the Lancia Stratos.

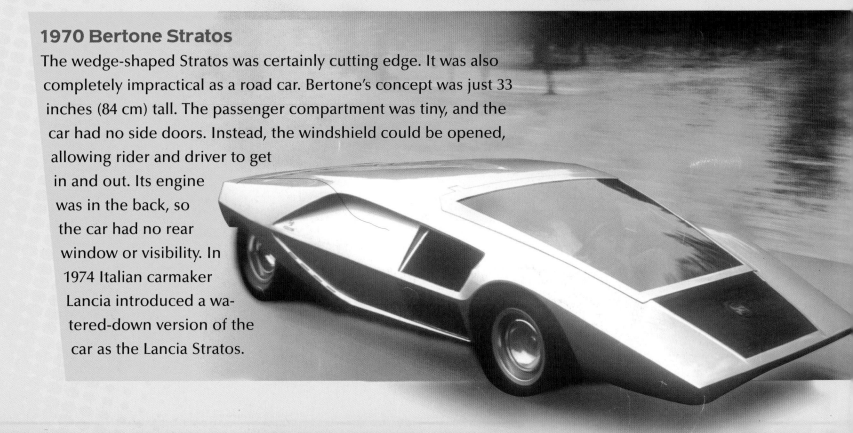

1995 Chrysler Atlantic

The Atlantic is a throwback to the elegant, high-priced European sports cars of the 1930s. In fact, it was named after a very rare classic French car, the Bugatti Atlantique. Legend has it that Chrysler president Bob Lutz came up with the idea at a gathering of classic car collectors. Lutz was wowed by the beautiful old cars on display. He sketched the idea for a similar, new car on a napkin.

2002 GM AUTOnomy

"AUTOnomy," says GM president Rick Wagoner, "[is] the start of a revolution in how automobiles are designed, built and used." All of AUTOnomy's major working parts—hydrogen fuel cell engines, onboard computer, and so on—are part of the car's 6-inch-thick (15 cm) skateboard (frame). Different bodies—a coupe or a station wagon, for example—can be easily attached to the skateboard. All driver controls, such as steering, brakes, and turn signals, can be controlled electronically.

2002 Cadillac Cien

Cien was Cadillac's vision of a high-powered sports car of the future. It won *AutoWeek* magazine's 2002 Best Concept Car award. The Cien's huge V12 engine is mounted near the center of the car. This layout is found on most high-priced supercars such as Lamborghinis and Ferraris. The mid-engine design gives the car better balance when turning at high speeds. The Cien also has such high-tech features as Night Vision, a system that allows drivers to see far ahead on the road after dark.

2005 Ford SYN^{US}

Ford's SYN^{US} concept was designed to be a tough city car of the future. It is built to be secure. When parked, shutters roll down to cover and protect the windows and windshield. The small windows on the side and roof are strong enough to stop bullets. Inside, the car has comfortable seating for four and a giant TV mounted in back. While driving, the TV screen works as a rear window, showing what's behind the car.

2005 Nissan Pivo

Who needs reverse when you can simply turn the whole passenger compartment around? Nissan's egg-shaped Pivo can do just that. The Pivo was designed to give the driver the most all-around visibility possible. It even has TV screens next to the windshield that show what is going on outside the car. The electric-powered car was also built to be very small and lightweight.

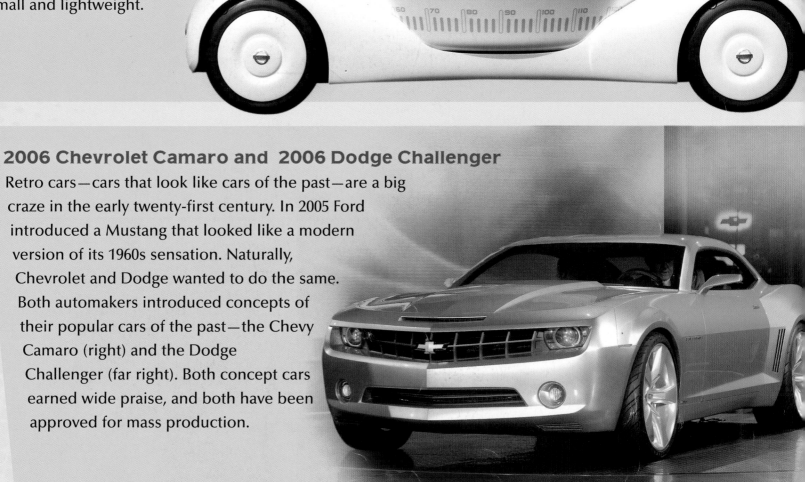

2006 Chevrolet Camaro and 2006 Dodge Challenger

Retro cars—cars that look like cars of the past—are a big craze in the early twenty-first century. In 2005 Ford introduced a Mustang that looked like a modern version of its 1960s sensation. Naturally, Chevrolet and Dodge wanted to do the same. Both automakers introduced concepts of their popular cars of the past—the Chevy Camaro (right) and the Dodge Challenger (far right). Both concept cars earned wide praise, and both have been approved for mass production.

Glossary

aerodynamic: shaped so that air flows easily over and around an object, such as a car

brand: a type of product made by a particular company with a particular name

buck: a basic frame, usually made of wood or foam, to which designers add clay to build models of car designs

CAD: computer-aided design. CAD programs turn two-dimensional images, such as drawings, into 3-D images that can be viewed from any angle.

canopy: the transparent plastic or glass covering of an aircraft's cockpit

coachwork: the specially built body, or exterior, of an automobile

coupe: a two-door car that usually seats only two people

model year: the particular year that a car is produced. For U.S. automakers, the model year begins a few months before the calendar year. For example, cars for the 1968 model year became widely available in late 1967.

retro: bringing to mind a style, fashion, or taste from the past

running board: a footboard below the door on the outside of an automobile. People step on the board to get into the vehicle.

tooling: equipping a factory with the tools needed to build and assemble an automobile

Selected Bibliography

Bell, Jonathan. *Concept Car Design: Driving the Dream*. Mies, Switzerland: RotoVision, 2003.

Buckley, Martin, and Chris Rees. *The World Encyclopedia of Cars: The Definitive Guide to Classic and Contemporary Cars from 1945 to 2000*. New York: Hermes House, 1999.

Coffey, Frank, and Joseph Layden. *America on Wheels: The First 100 Years: 1896–1996*. Los Angeles: General Publishing Group, 1996.

DeLorenzo, Matt. *American Cars: Past to Present*. New York: Barnes and Noble Books, 2004.

Dredge, Richard. *Concept Cars: Designing for the Future*. San Diego: Thunder Bay Press, 2004.

Edsall, Larry. *Concept Cars: From the 1930s to the Present*. New York: Barnes and Noble Books, 2003.

Heilig, John. *Detroit Dream Cars*. Saint Paul: MBI Publishing Company, 2001.

Rees, Chris. *Concept Cars: An A–Z Guide of the World's Most Fabulous Futuristic Cars*. New York: Barnes and Noble Books, 2000.

Willson, Quentin. *Cars: A Celebration*. New York: Dorling Kindersley, 2001.

Further Reading

Doeden, Matt. *Crazy Cars*. Minneapolis: Lerner Publications Company, 2007.

Mueller, Mike. *The Corvette*. Saint Paul: Crestline, 2003.

Websites

Car Design News
http://www.cardesignnews.com/
This site features photos of the latest concepts and new production cars, as well as news from the major auto shows.

Car Show News
http://carshownews.com
This handy site includes a calendar that lists the names, dates, and locations of hundreds of car shows across the country.

Official Harley Earl Website
http://www.carofthecentury.com/
Learn more about GM design wizard Harley Earl from his official website. The site features information on Earl's life, his impact on the automobile industry, and photos of his most famous cars.

Index

About the Author

Jeffrey Zuehlke is a writer and editor. He has written more than a dozen nonfiction books for children. He lives in Minneapolis, Minnesota.

About the Consutant

Mike Mueller is an automotive writer and photographer. He has written and photographed more than 30 books on automotive history. He lives in Atlanta, Georgia.

Photo Acknowledgments

The images in this book are used with the permission of: © Dean Siracusa/TRAN-STOCK, pp. 4-5, 18; Photo Courtesy of National Automobile Museum (The Harrah Collection), p. 6; © Mike Mueller, pp. 6 (background), 7, 9, 16, 38 (top), 39 (top); © Getty Images, pp. 8, 32, 33, 36 (bottom), 37 (bottom), 43 (both), 44 (both); © Bettmann/CORBIS, pp. 10, 13; Copyright 2006 GM Corp. Used with permission GM Media Archive, pp. 11, 15, 22 (background), 31, 40 (bottom), 41 (bottom); www.ronkimballstock.com, p. 12; From the Collections of The Henry Ford, p. 14; © Science Museum/SSPL/The Image Works, p. 17; © Reuter Raymond/Corbis Sygma, p. 19; © Reuters/CORBIS, p. 20; © Leilani Hu/ZUMA Press, p. 22 (bottom); © Hank Morgan/Photo Researchers, Inc., p. 23; © Artemis Images/ATD Group, Inc., p. 24 (top); © Martyn Goddard/TRANSTOCK, pp. 24 (bottom), 38 (bottom), 39 (bottom); Courtesy College for Creative Studies, pp. 25, 29 (left), 30; © Maximilian Stock Ltd/Photo Researchers, Inc., p. 26; © Peter Yates/Photo Researchers, Inc., p. 27; Photo R Meinert © Neill Bruce, p. 28; © Slavko Midzor/JLP/ZUMA Press, p. 29 (right); © Glenn Paulina/TRANSTOCK, pp. 34 (top), 35 (top); © John Lamm/TRANSTOCK, pp. 34 (bottom), 35 (bottom); © Ron Perry/TRAN-STOCK, pp. 36 (top), 37 (top); AP Images/Heribert Proepper, p. 40 (top); Copyright DaimlerChrysler Corporation. Used with Permission, p. 41 (top); © Guy Spangenberg/TRANSTOCK, p. 42 (top); © Jim West/ZUMA Press, p. 42 (bottom); © Issei Kato/Reuters/Corbis, p. 45 (top); © Jim West/The Image Works, p. 45 (bottom).

Front cover: www.ronkimballstock.com